ESL Phonics
for All Ages

Book 1
Beginning Consonants

by

Elizabeth Claire

Illustrations by

Joe Frazier
and
Dave Nicholson

Developmental Editor: Nancy Baxer
Editorial Consultant: Marilyn Rosenthal
Copy Editors: Nadine Simms, Devra Weingart
Design: Steve Jorgensen
Layout: Dr. Andrew Sachs
Illustrations: Joe Frazier and Dave Nicholson
Cover Design: Elizabeth Claire
Cover Photo: Corbis Photos

Published by: Eardley Publications
Saddle Brook, NJ 07663 USA

Printed in the United States of America

ISBN: 978-0937630-13-6

CONTENTS
Book 1: Beginning Consonants

Each unit presents two consonant sounds with eight common examples. The two consonants are then contrasted for recall and production. Following that the words just learned are used in simple sentences with high frequency sight words. Each unit has a conversation, song, poem, or chant to practice phonics in meaningful, whole-language contexts.

Let's Begin

1.  look

2.  listen

3.  say

4.  read

5.  write

6.  draw

7.  circle

8.  find

9.  sing

10.  chant

11.  Check your work.

These words all begin with the sound /b/.

Listen to the words.

Say the words.

Write the letter **b** at the beginning of each word.

1. ____ us

2. ____ ook

3. ____ ird

4. ____ ananas

5. ____ ag

6. ____ aby

7. ____ ox

8. ____ oots

ESL Phonics for All Ages   Book 1   © Elizabeth Claire 2007   Unit 1

These words all begin with the sound /t/.

👂 Listen to the words.

🗣 Say the words.

✏️ Write the letter **t** at the beginning of each word.

1. _____ able

2. _____ elephone

3. _____ en 10

4. _____ oes

5. _____ urtle

6. _____ eeth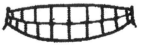

7. _____ eacher

8. _____ ea

👂 Listen and ✏️ Write

👂 Listen to the words.

🗣️ Say the words.

Do the words begin with the sound /b/ or /t/ ?

✏️ Write the letter **b** or **t** at the beginning of each word.

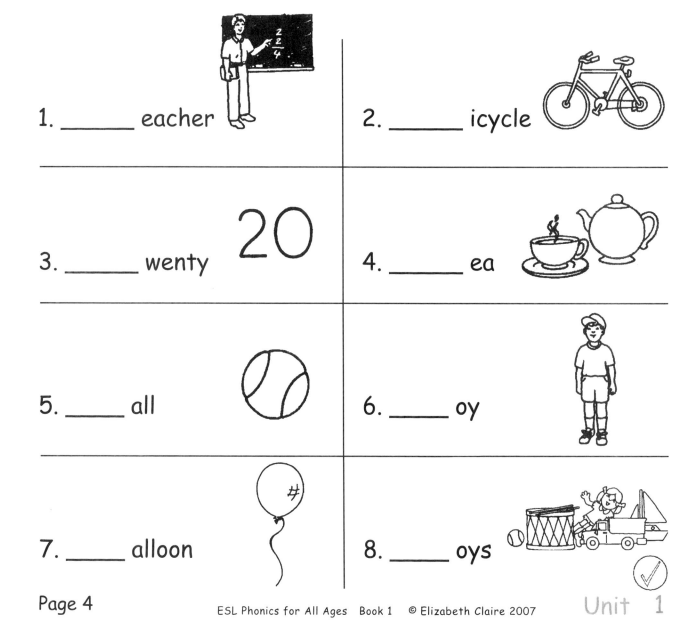

1. _____ eacher

2. _____ icycle

3. _____ wenty

4. _____ ea

5. _____ all

6. _____ oy

7. _____ alloon

8. _____ oys

Listen, Find, and Circle

Listen to the word.

Find a word that is the same.

Draw a circle around the same word.

1. teacher	table	toys	(teacher)	teeth
2. book	ball	baby	boy	book
3. bus	book	bus	bananas	bag
4. table	table	tea	turtle	telephone
5. bicycle	bird	baby	bananas	bicycle
6. toes	toys	tea	toes	ten

Happy Birthday, Big Boy!

Happy birthday, big boy!

Happy birthday, big boy!

Happy birthday, my baby,

Happy birthday, big boy!

1.   I have a book.

---

2.   I have a telephone.

---

3.    I have a bird.

---

4.   I have a turtle.

---

5.   I have a baby.

---

6.   I have a tooth.

Read and Find

1. (I have a tooth.)

2. (I have a book.)

3. (I have a turtle.)

4. (I have a baby.)

5. (I have a bird.)

6. (I have a telephone.)

Unit   1

 Read and Draw

1. I have a tooth.

2. I have a bird.

3. I have a table.

4. I have a baby.

5. I have a balloon.

6. I have a telephone.

S   S   S   ___   ___   ___

These words all begin with the sound /s/.

Listen to the words.

Say the words.

Write the letter **S** at the beginning of each word.

1. ____ ix **6**	2. ____ un 
3. ____ andwich	4. ____ alt 
5. ____ even **7**	6. ____ ink 
7. ____ ock 	8. ____ oup 

ESL Phonics for All Ages   Book 1   © Elizabeth Claire 2007   Unit 2

n n n

These words all begin with the sound /n/.

Listen to the words.

Say the words.

Write the letter **n** at the beginning of each word.

1. ____ ine **9**	2. ____ ose
3. ____ otebook	4. ____ urse
5. ____ umbers 2184 9573	6. ____ ight
7. ____ ame JOE	8. ____ eck

👂 Listen and ✏️ Write

👂 Listen to the words.

🐜 Say the words.

Do the words begin with the sound /s/ or /n/?

✏️ Write **s** or **n** at the beginning of each word.

1. _____ ewspaper

2. _____ est

3. _____ ing

4. _____ ineteen

5. _____ ofa

6. _____ alad

7. _____ oap

8. _____ ickel

ESL Phonics for All Ages   Book 1   © Elizabeth Claire 2007

Unit 2

Listen, Find, and Circle

○ Listen to the word.   ○ Find the same word.

○ Draw a circle around the same word.

6				
1. six	seven	sink	six	sun
2. sandwich	sandwich	salt	soup	sock
3. nose	nose	notebook	nurse	name
4. numbers	nineteen	newspaper	numbers	night
5. sock	soup	sofa	soap	sock
6. neck	name	neck	nest	nickel

  **Listen and**  **Read**

1. May I have a sandwich, please?

2. May I have some soup, please?

3. May I have some salad, please?

4. May I have a notebook, please?

5. May I have a newspaper, please?

6. May I have a nickel, please?

Tuna Sandwich

Tuna sandwich hot,
Tuna sandwich cold.
My tuna sandwich
Is ten days old!

I like it hot.
You like it cold.
Nobody likes it when
It's ten days old!

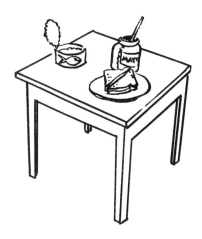

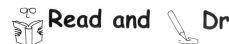 # Read and Draw

1. I have a sandwich.

2. I have a notebook.

3. I have a sock.

4. I have a nose.

5. I have a neck.

6. I have a sofa.

👂 Listen and ✏️ Write

👂 Listen to the words.

🗣️ Say the words.

✏️ Write **s** or **n** or **b** or **t** at the beginning of each word.

1. ____ ird

2. ____ un

3. ____ eeth

4. ____ ose

5. ____ andwich

6. ____ elephone

7. ____ umbers

8. ____ ox

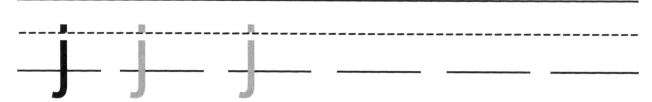

j ⎺j⎺ ⎺j⎺ ⎺ ⎺ ⎺

These words all begin with the sound /j/.

Listen to the words.

Say the words.

Write the letter **j** at the beginning of each word.

1. ____ et

2. ____ acket

3. ____ ug

4. ____ ail

5. ____ am

6. ____ uice

7. ____ ack-in-the-box

8. ____ ar

ESL Phonics for All Ages Book 1 © Elizabeth Claire 2007

r r r r _____ _____ _____ _____

These words all begin with the sound /r/.

Listen to the words.

Say the words.

Write the letter **r** at the beginning of each word.

1. ____ ain

2. ____ ice

3. ____ uler

4. ____ abbit

5. ____ at

6. ____ ock

7. ____ ug

8. ____ oof

👂 Listen and ✎ Write

👂 Listen to the words.

🕷 Say the words.

Do the words begin with the sound /j/ or the /r/?

✎ Write **j** or **r** at the beginning of each word.

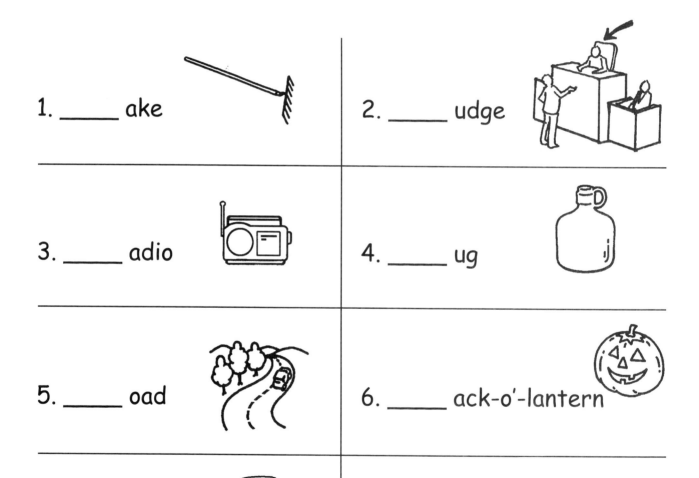

1. ____ ake

2. ____ udge

3. ____ adio

4. ____ ug

5. ____ oad

6. ____ ack-o'-lantern

7. ____ eans

8. ____ ing

ESL Phonics for All Ages   Book 1   © Elizabeth Claire 2007   Unit   3

Listen, Find, and ◯ Circle

👂 Listen to the word. ☝ Find the same word.

◯ Draw a circle around the same word.

1. jam	jug	jail	jar	jam
2. jet	jet	jacket	juice	jar
3. jug	jar	jug	juice	jam
4. rat	rug	rake	ring	rat
5. rug	jug	rug	road	rake
6. ruler	radio	jumper	ruler	rock

Jingle Bells

Jingle bells, jingle bells, jingle all the way!

Oh what fun it is to ride

In a one-horse open sleigh. Oh,

Jingle bells, jingle bells, jingle all the way!

Oh what fun it is to ride

In a one-horse open sleigh!

 Listen and  Read

 1. This is my jacket.

2. This is my ring.

 3. This is my jack-o'-lantern.

4. This is my rice.

5. This is my rug.

 6. This is my jug.

 **Read and Draw**

1. This is my rabbit.

2. This is my jack-o'lantern.

3. This is my jacket.

4. This is my radio.

5. This is my jug.

6. This is my ring.

ESL Phonics for All Ages   Book 1   © Elizabeth Claire 2007   Unit   3

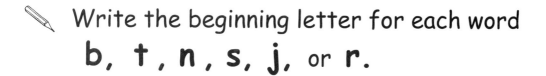 Say and ✎ Write

👓 Look at the pictures. Say the words.

What's the beginning sound?

✎ Write the beginning letter for each word
b, t, n, s, j, or **r.**

1. ____ acket	2. ____ ine
3. ____ andwich	4. ____ eeth
5. ____ ird	6. ____ eck
7. ____ elephone	8. ____ ox

👂 Listen and ✏️ Write

👂 Listen to each word.

What's the beginning sound?

✏️ Write the letter **b**, **t**, **n**, **s**, **j**, or **r**.

1. _b_ ananas	2. ___ even	3. ___ ar
4. ___ en	5. ___ oes	6. ___ ickel
7. ___ adio	8. ___ un	9. ___ ook
10. ___ eck	11. ___ uler	12. ___ est
13. ___ ug	14. ___ all	15. ___ eeth
16. ___ ock	17. ___ iger	18. ___ et
19. ___ icycle	20. ___ ea	21. ___ ose

⚲ Find the Same Word

👓 Look at the words.

✎ Draw a line to the words that are the same.

1. ring   rice

2. rice   road

3. road   ring

4. jet   jacket

5. jacket   jet

6. jam   rat

7. rat   ruler

8. ruler   jam

p p p ___ ___ ___

These words all begin with the sound /p/.

Listen to the words.

Say the words.

Write the letter **p** at the beginning of each word.

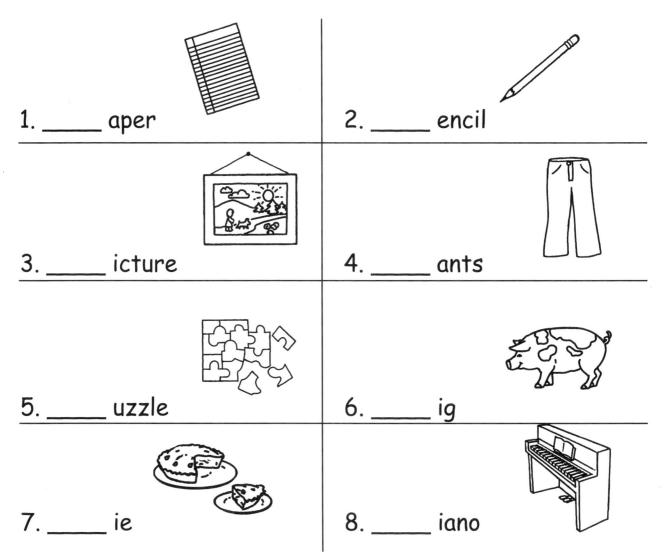

1. _____ aper

2. _____ encil

3. _____ icture

4. _____ ants

5. _____ uzzle

6. _____ ig

7. _____ ie

8. _____ iano

ESL Phonics for All Ages Book 1   © Elizabeth Claire 2007   Unit 4

C _ C _ C _ _ _ _ _ _

These words all begin with the sound /k/.

Listen to the words.

Say the words.

Write the letter **C** at the beginning of each word.

1. _____ at

2. _____ ow

3. _____ up

4. _____ oat

5. _____ alendar

6. _____ arrot

7. _____ ookie

8. _____ ar

👂 Listen and ✏️ Write

👂 Listen to the words.

🕷️ Say the words.

Do the words begin with the sound /p/ or /k/?

✏️ Write **p** or **c** at the beginning of each word.

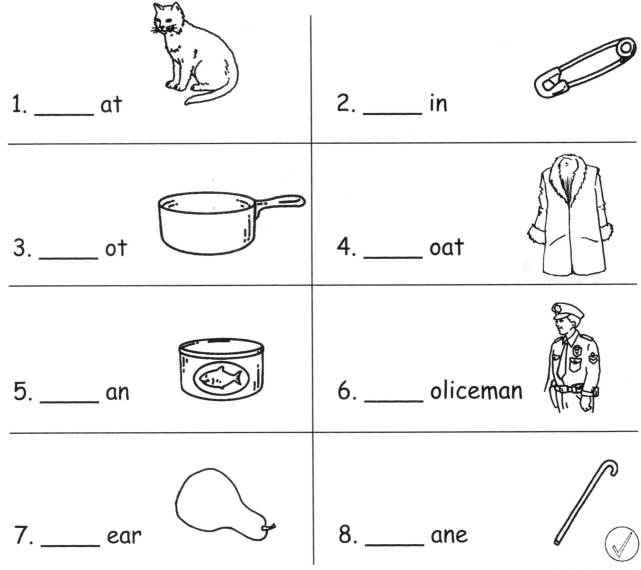

1. _____ at

2. _____ in

3. _____ ot

4. _____ oat

5. _____ an

6. _____ oliceman

7. _____ ear

8. _____ ane

ESL Phonics for All Ages   Book 1   © Elizabeth Claire 2007   Unit 4

Listen and 👓 Read

1. She has a cat.

2. She has a puzzle.

3. She has a calendar.

4. He has a carrot.

5. He has a pig.

6. He has a picture.

Listen, Find, and Circle

Listen to the word. Read the word.
Draw a circle around the same word.

1. pig	picture	pan	piano	(pig)
2. picture	piano	pencil	picture	pie
3. puzzle	pants	pear	puzzle	piano
4. cat	cup	coat	cat	car
5. carrot	cat	cup	carrot	car
6. calendar	cat	cow	calendar	cane

ESL Phonics for All Ages   Book 1   © Elizabeth Claire 2007   Unit   4

1. She has a cat.

2. She has a puzzle.

3. She has a calendar.

4. He has a carrot.

5. He has a pig.

6. He has a picture.

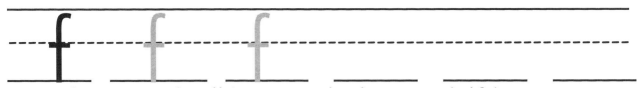

f _ f _ f _ _ _ _ _ _

These words all begin with the sound /f/.

Listen to the words.

Say the words.

Write the letter **f** at the beginning of each word.

1. ____ oot

2. ____ ace

3. ____ ive 5

4. ____ our 4

5. ____ ish

6. ____ amily

7. ____ inger

8. ____ lag

 ESL Phonics for All Ages   Book 1   © Elizabeth Claire 2007 Unit 5

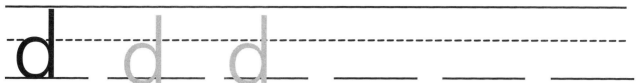
d _d_ _d_ _____ _____ _____

These words all begin with the sound /d/.

 Listen to the words.

Say the words.

Write the letter **d** at the beginning of each word.

1. _____ esk 	2. _____ oor 
3. _____ ollar 	4. _____ ime
5. _____ og 	6. _____ ish 
7. _____ eer 	8. _____ uck 

👂 Listen and ✏️ Write

👂 Listen to the words.

Say the words.

Do you hear the sound /f/ or the sound /d/?

✏️ Write **f** or **d** at the beginning of each word.

1. ____ ootball

2. ____ ifty 50

3. ____ oor

4. ____ oll

5. ____ ather

6. ____ ancer

7. ___ eet

8. ___ irty

ESL Phonics for All Ages   Book 1   © Elizabeth Claire 2007   Unit 5

Listen and Read

1. What do you have?

2. We have a football.

---

3. What do you have?

4. We have a fish.

---

5. What do you have?

6. We have a dog.

---

7. What do you have?

8. We have a dollar.

Read and **Find**

What do you have?

1. We have a fish.

2. We have a dog.

3. We have a doll.

4. We have a dollar.

5. We have a football.

Bingo

There is a farmer

And he has a dog

And Bingo is his name, oh!

B-i-n-g-o

B-i-n-g-o

B-i-n-g-o

And Bingo is his name, oh!

m m m

These words all begin with the sound /m/.

 Listen to the words.

Say the words.

Write the letter **m** at the beginning of each word.

1. _____ an

2. _____ ap

3. _____ ilk

4. _____ outh

5. _____ oney

6. _____ itten

7. _____ onkey

8. _____ om

ESL Phonics for All Ages   Book 1   © Elizabeth Claire 2007

Unit 6

These words all begin with the sound /l/.

Listen to the words.

Say the words.

Write the letter **l** at the beginning of each word.

1. _____ eg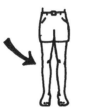

2. _____ ion

3. _____ emon

4. _____ eaf

5. _____ ock

6. _____ ips

7. _____ unch

8. _____ etters

👂 Listen and ✏️ Write

👂 Listen to the words.

🗣️ Say the words.

Do the words begin with the sound /l/ or /m/?

✏️ Write **l** or **m** at the beginning of each word.

1. _____ ouse	2. _____ ask
3. _____ amp	4. _____ ion
5. _____ ailbox	6. _____ ock
7. _____ ips	8. _____ oon

ESL Phonics for All Ages Book 1   © Elizabeth Claire 2007

Unit 6

1. What do they have?

2. They have a mouse and a lion.

3. What do they have?

4. They have a map and a lamp.

5. What do they have?

6. They have lunch and milk.

7. What do they have?

8. They have money and a lock.

What do they have?

1. They have a mouse and a lion.

2. They have a map and a lamp.

3. They have lunch and milk.

4. They have money and a lock.

# Read and Draw

1. They have milk.

2. They have money and a map.

3. They have a lamp and a lock.

4. They have a mouse.

5. They have lunch.

6. They have a lion.

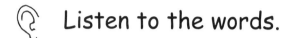

These words all begin with the sound /v/.

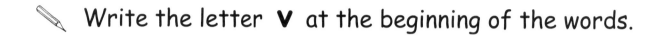 Listen to the words.

Say the words.

Write the letter **V** at the beginning of the words.

1. _____ an

2. _____ egetables

3. _____ olleyball

4. _____ est

5. _____ olcano

6. _____ acuum cleaner

7. _____ iolin

8. _____ ase

ESL Phonics for All Ages   Book 1   © Elizabeth Claire 2007   Unit 7

Z Z Z ___ ___ ___

These words all begin with the sound /z/.

 Listen to the words.

Say the words.

✏️ Write the letter **Z** at the beginning of the words.

1. ____ ero   O123

2. ____ ebra

3. ____ ip code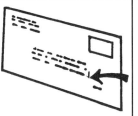

4. ____ ipper

5. ____ oo

Listen and Write

Listen to the words.

Say the words.

Do the words begin with the sound /v/ or /z/?

Write **V** or **Z** at the beginning of each word.

1. ____ iolet 	2. ____ ipper 
3. ____ acuum cleaner 	4. ____ alley 
5. ____ itamin 	6. ____ ero 0123
7. ____ iolin 	8. ____ isitor 

ESL Phonics for All Ages   Book 1   © Elizabeth Claire 2007   Unit 7

Roses are Red

Roses are red,

Violets are blue.

Sugar is sweet,

And so are you.

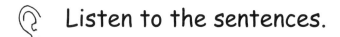
 Listen to the sentences.

Read the sentences.

---

1. The man is eating lunch.

---

2. The dog is eating a fish.

---

3. The policeman is eating a lemon.

---

4. The monkey is eating a pie.

---

5. The pig is eating vegetables.

👂 Listen and ✏️ Write

👂 Listen to the sentences.

What letters are missing?

✏️ Write the beginning sounds.

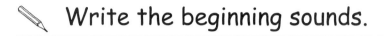

1. The____ig is eating ____egetables.

2. The ____ oliceman is eating a ____ emon.

3. The ____ an is eating ____ unch.

4. The ____ og is eating a ____ ish.

5. The ____ onkey is eating a ____ ie.

Listen and Read

1. Take the violets
   from the valley.

2. Put the violets
   in the vase.

3. Take the volleyball
   from the visitor.

4. Put the volleyball
   in the van.

5. Take the vegetables
   from the bag.

6. Put the vegetables
   in the pot.

ESL Phonics for All Ages   Book 1   © Elizabeth Claire 2007   Unit 7

# Read and Draw

1. A dog is eating a fish.

2. A man is eating a duck.

3. A pig is eating vegetables.

4. A boy is eating a lemon.

5. A zebra is eating a leaf.

6. A fish is eating a volleyball.

👂 Listen and ✏️ Write

👂 Listen to each word.

What's the beginning sound?

✏️ Write **p**, **c**, **d**, **f**, **l**, **m**, **v** or **z**.

1. ____ encil	2. ____ inger	3. ____ ap
4. ____ egetables	5. ____ outh	6. ____ at
7. ____ ig	8. ____ an	9. ____ oney
10. ____ oot	11. ____ uck	12. ____ ero
13. ____ ipper	14. ____ oor	15. ____ icture
16. ____ olcano	17. ____ ish	18. ____ ar
19. ____ ootball	20. ____ ouse	21. ____ oll

ESL Phonics for All Ages Book 1   © Elizabeth Claire 2007   Unit 7 ✓

g g g _____ _____ _____

The letter g makes two sounds: /j/ and /g/.

These words all begin with the sound /j/.

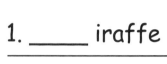 Listen to the words. Say the words.

Write the letter **g** at the beginning of each word.

1. _____ iraffe

2. _____ iant

3. _____ enie

4. _____ ingerbread man

5. _____ ym

Row, Row, Row, Your Boat

Row, row, row, your boat,

Gently down the stream!

Merrily, merrily, merrily, merrily,

Life is but a dream!

👂 Listen and ✏️ Write

These words all begin with the sound /g/.

👂 Listen to the words.

🗣️ Say the words.

✏️ Write the letter **g** at the beginning of each word.

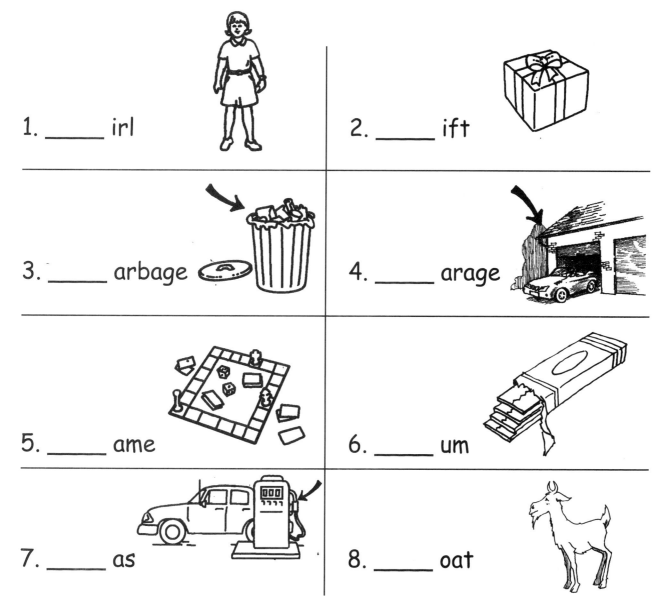

1. _____ irl

2. _____ ift

3. _____ arbage

4. _____ arage

5. _____ ame

6. _____ um

7. _____ as

8. _____ oat

h

The letter h makes the sound /h/.

👂 Listen to the words. 🐝 Say the words.

✏️ Write the letter **h** at the beginning of each word.

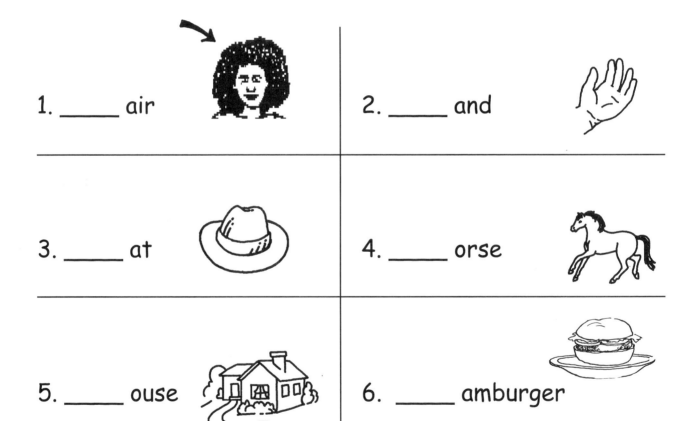

1. _____ air

2. _____ and

3. _____ at

4. _____ orse

5. _____ ouse

6. _____ amburger

7. _____ ot dog

8. _____ eart

Listen and ✎ Write

Listen to the words.

Say the words.

Do the words begin with the sound /g/, /j/, or /h/?

✎ Write the letter **g** or **h** at the beginning of these words.

1. ___g___ ift

2. ___g___ as

3. ___h___ and

4. ___g___ arbage

5. ____ at

6. ____ eart

7. ____ ame

8. ____ ill

1. Hi!

2. Hello!

3. How are you?

4. I'm fine, thank you.
   How are you?

5. I'm fine, thank you.

6. So long.

7. Good bye.

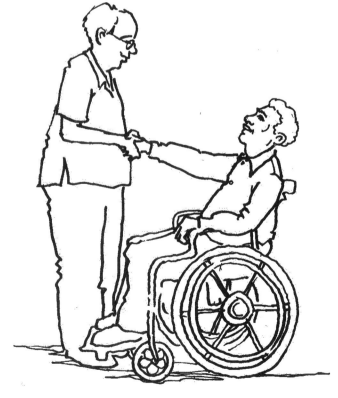

☊ Listen, ☌ Find, and ○ Circle

☊ Listen to the word. 📖 Read the word.
○ Draw a circle around the same word.

1. girl	gift	game	_girl_	gas	
2. house	horse	_house_	hair	hat	
3. heart	hat	head	hen	_heart_	
4. game	_game_	goat	genie	garbage	
5. hat	hair	hand	_hat_	hamburger	
6. giant	game	girl	_giant_	giraffe	✓

The letter **C** makes two sounds: /k/ and /s/.

C makes the sound /s/ before e, i, and y.

 Listen to the words. Say the words.

Write the letter **C** at the beginning of the words.

1. ___ ircle

2. ___ ent

3. ___ eiling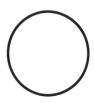

4. ___ enter

5. ___ ity

W   W   W

The letter **W** makes the sound /w/.

These words all begin with the sound /w/.

Listen to the words. Say the words.

Write the letter **W** at the beginning of the words.

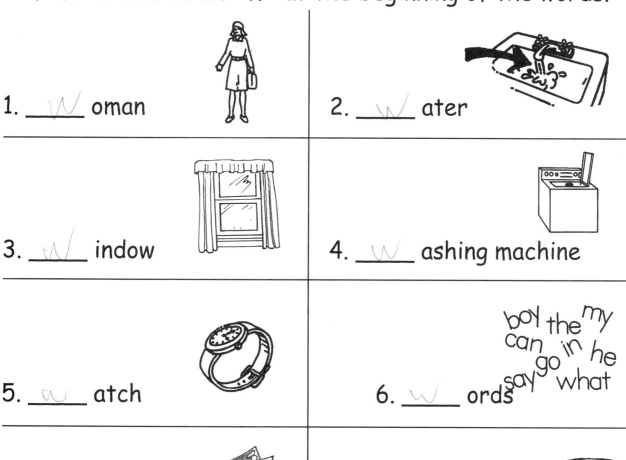

1. __W__ oman

2. __W__ ater

3. __W__ indow

4. __W__ ashing machine

5. __W__ atch

6. __W__ ords

7. __W__ allet

8. __W__ astebasket

👂 Listen and ✏️ Write

👂 Listen to the words.

🗣️ Say the words.

Do the words begin with the sound /w/, /s/ or /k/?

✏️ Write **W** or **C** at the beginning of each word.

1. ___c___ ar

2. ___w___ ater

3. ___w___ agon

4. ___w___ olf

5. ___c___ orn

6. ___c___ ity

7. ___c___ ircle

8. ___c___ offee

ESL Phonics for All Ages   Book 1   © Elizabeth Claire 2007

Unit 9

1. Can you see a woman?	(Yes)	No
2. Can you see a cup?	Yes	(No)
3. Can you see a cow?	(Yes)	No
4. Can you see a city?	(Yes)	No
5. Can you see a wagon?	(Yes)	No
6. Can you see a wolf?	(Yes)	No

👂 Listen and ✏️ Write

👂 Listen to the words.

✏️ Write the beginning sounds of the words.

Write **c**, **g**, **h**, or **w**.

1. _c_ at	2. _g_ oman	3. _h_ orse
4. _g_ iant	5. _w_ ill	6. _c_ up
7. _h_ eart	8. _g_ ym	9. _w_ ater
10. _g_ iant	11. _c_ atch	12. _h_ ouse
13. _c_ ircle	14. _h_ ow	15. _y_ ard
16. _c_ alendar	17. _w_ ent	18. _g_ iraffe
19. _c_ ity	20. _w_ indow	21. _c_ air

ESL Phonics for All Ages Book 1   © Elizabeth Claire 2007   Unit 9

Listen to the sentences.

Write the beginning sounds of the words.

Write **c**, **g**, **h**, or **w**.

1. The ___girl is looking at a ___ ame.

2. The ___ iant is looking at a ___ enie.

3. The ___ oman is looking at a ___ oat.

4. The ___ at is looking at a ___ amburger.

5. The ___ ow is looking at some ___ ater.

k k k ___ ___ ___

The letter k makes the sound /k/.

These words all begin with the sound /k/.

 Listen to the words. Say the words.

Write the letter **k** at the beginning of the words.

1. __k_ ing

2. ___ ite

3. __k_ itten

4. __k_ ey

5. __k_ ettle

6. __k_ angaroo

7. __k_ iss

ESL Phonics for All Ages Book 1 © Elizabeth Claire 2007   Unit 10

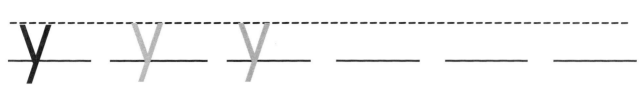

y   y   y

The letter y makes the sound /y/.

These words all begin with the sound /y/.

Listen to the words. Say the words.

Write the letter **y** at the beginning of the words.

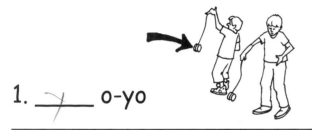

1. __y__ o-yo

2. __y__ ak

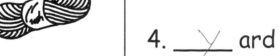

3. __y__ arn

4. __y__ ard

5. __y__ olk

6. __y__ acht

7. __y__ awn

8. __y__ ellow

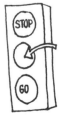

👂 Listen and ✏️ Write

👂 Listen to the words.

🗣️ Say the words.

Do the words begin with the sound /k/ or /y/?

✏️ Write **k** or **y** at the beginning of each word.

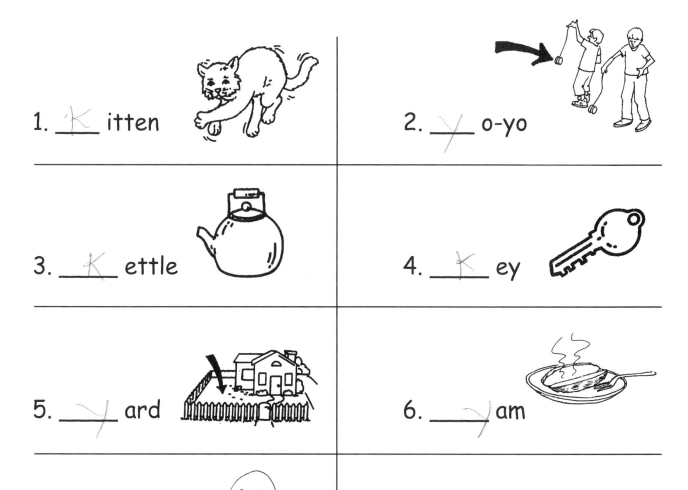

1. __K__ itten

2. __y__ o-yo

3. __K__ ettle

4. __K__ ey

5. __y__ ard

6. __y__ am

7. __K__ iss

ESL Phonics for All Ages   Book 1   © Elizabeth Claire 2007   Unit 10

Listen and  Read

 Listen to the sentences.

Read the sentences.

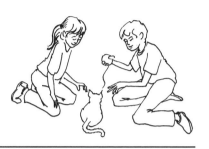

1. They are playing with a kitten.

2. They are playing with a kite.

3. They are playing with yo-yos.

4. They are playing with a key.

ch

These words all begin with the sound /ch/.

 Listen to the words.

Say the words.

Write the letters **ch** at the beginning of the words.

1. _c_ _h_ air

2. _c_ _h_ ildren

3. _c_ _h_ alk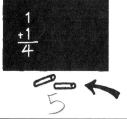

4. _c_ _h_ eese

5. _c_ _h_ eek

6. _c_ _h_ eck

7. _c_ _h_ erries

8. _c_ _h_ icken

ESL Phonics for All Ages   Book 1   © Elizabeth Claire 2007   Unit 11

These words all begin with the sound /th/.

Listen to the words.

Say the words.

Write the letters **th** at the beginning of the words.

1. _Th_ umb

2. _Th_ ief

3. _Th_ irty 30

4. _Th_ ousand 1,000

5. _Th_ irteen 13

6. _Th_ ursday

Sun	Mon	Tues	Wed	Thur	Fri	Sat
					1	2
3	4	5	6	7	8	9
10	11	12	13	14	15	16
17	18	19	20	21	22	23
24/31	25	26	27	28	29	30

7. _Th_ ermometer

👂Listen and ✏️ Write

👂 Listen to the words.

🗣️ Say the words.

Do you hear the sound /th/ or /ch/ ?

✏️ Write **th** or **ch** at the beginning of the words.

1. ___ ___ air

2. ___ ___ umb

3. ___ ___ irty 30

4. ___ ___ ousand 1,000

5. ___ ___ icken

6. ___ ___ ildren

7. ___ ___ ermometer

Thank You

Thank you, thank you, thank you.

A thousand times, I thank you.

Thank you for the chickens.

Thank you for the cheese.

Thank you for the cherries,

Thank you for all of these.

You're welcome!

qu 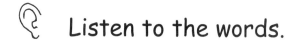 qu qu _____ _____ _____

The letters qu make the sound /kw/.

Listen to the words.

Say the words.

✎ Write the letters **qu** at the beginning of the words.

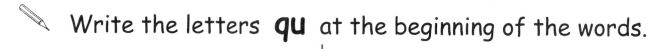

1. _q_ _u_ een

2. _q_ _u_ arter

3. _q_ _u_ estion mark

4. _q_ _u_ art

5. _q_ _u_ ilt

6. _q_ _u_ iz

Listen and 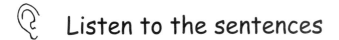Read

 Listen to the sentences

Read the sentences.

1. He is drawing a chair.

---

2. He is drawing a chicken.

---

3. She is drawing a quilt.
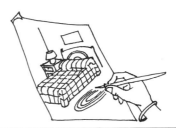

---

4. He is drawing a quarter.

---

5. She is drawing a queen.

👂 Listen and ✏️ Write

👂 Listen to the words.

🗣️ Say the words.

Do you hear the sound /th/, /ch/ or /kw/ ?

✏️ Write **th**, **ch**, or **qu** at the beginning of the words.

Sun	Mon	Tues	Wed	Thur	Fri	Sat
					1	2
3	4	5	6	7	8	9
10	11	12	13	14	15	16
17	18	19	20	21	22	23
24/31	25	26	27	28	29	30

1. _c_ _h_ eek

2. _Th_ ursday

3. _q_ _u_ ueen

4. _Th_ irteen **13**

5. _c_ _h_ eck ✓

6. _c_ _h_ eese

7. _q_ _u_ art

8. _K_ _u_ iz

ESL Phonics for All Ages   Book 1   © Elizabeth Claire 2007   Unit 11

Ⓛ Listen and ✎ Write

Ⓛ Listen to the words.

✎ Write the beginning sounds of the words.

Use **th, ch,** or **qu.**

1. _ch_ ildren	2. _Th_ een	3. _Th_ irty
4. _qu_ art	5. _ch_ air	6. _s ?_ eek
7. _Th_ ousand	8. _ch_ erries	9. _ch_ umb
10. _Ch_ icken	11. _qu_ arter	12. _ch_ ilt
13. _ch_ iz	14. _qu_ ief	15. _Th_ irteen
16. _ch_ eck	17. _qu_ estion	18. _Th_ ermometer

sh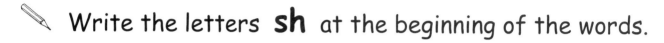

These words all begin with the sound /sh/.

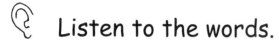 Listen to the words.

Say the words.

Write the letters **sh** at the beginning of the words.

1. _____ _____ irt

2. _____ _____ eep

3. _____ _____ oe

4. _____ _____ ovel

5. _____ _____ ell

6. _____ _____ ark

7. _____ _____ ip

8. _____ _____ adow

ESL Phonics for All Ages   Book 1   © Elizabeth Claire 2007   Unit 12

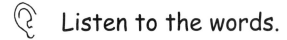

wh wh wh ___ ___ ___

These words all begin with the sound /hw/.

Listen to the words.

Say the words.

Write the letters **wh** at the beginning of the words.

1. ___ ___ eel 	2. ___ ___ ale
3. ___ ___ ip	4. ___ ___ isker
5. ___ ___ eelbarrow 	6. ___ ___ istle

👂 Listen and ✏️ Write

👂 Listen to the words.

🕷️ Say the words.

Do you hear the sound /sh/ or /wh/ ?

✏️ Write **sh**, or **wh**, at the beginning of the words.

1. ___ ___ irt

2. ___ ___ eel

3. ___ ___ oe

4. ___ ale

5. ___ ___ isker

6. ___ ___ ark

7. ___ ___ ip

8. ___ ___ istle

ESL Phonics for All Ages   Book 1   © Elizabeth Claire 2007

Unit 12 ✓

Listen and Read

 Listen to the sentences. Read the sentences.

1. Where's the wheel? There it is. It's number 1.	2. Where's the shark? There it is. It's number 2.
3. Where's the whale? There it is. It's number 3.	4. Where's the shoe? There it is. It's number 4.
5. Where's the shirt? There it is. It's number 5.	6. Where's the whistle? There it is. It's number 6.

Read and ○ Find

 Read the sentences.

○ Find the things in the picture. Write the number.

1. Where's the whistle?
    It's number __.
	2. Where's the shoe?
	    It's number __.

3. Where's the shirt?
    It's number __.
	4. Where's the whale?
	    It's number __.

5. Where's the shark?
    It's number __.
	6. Where's the wheel?
	    It's number __.

ESL Phonics for All Ages   Book 1   © Elizabeth Claire 2007   Unit 12

Where is my dog?

Where, oh where
 has my little dog gone?

Oh where, oh where
 can he be?

With his tail cut short
 and his ears cut long—

Oh where,
 oh where
 has he gone?

Look and Write

Look at the pictures.

Say the words.

What is the beginning sound?

Write the letter at the beginning of each word.

1. ___ ox

2. ___ able

3. ___ ock

4. ___ ose

5. ___ ar

6. ___ uler

7. ___ ants

8. ___ ar

ESL Phonics for All Ages   Book 1   © Elizabeth Claire 2007

Test

👓 Look and ✏ Write

👓 Look at the pictures.

🐛 Say the words.

What is the beginning sound?

✏ Write the letter at the beginning of each word.

1. ___ ish

2. ___ oor

3. ___ oney

4. ___ unch

5. ___ an

6. ___ ipper

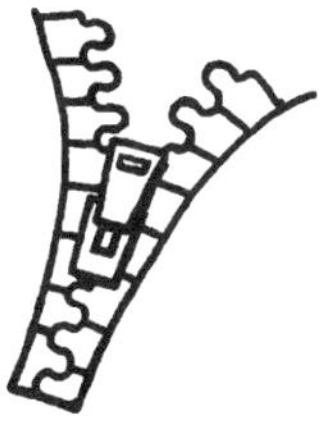

7. ___ ym

8. ___ irl

ᓂ Look and ✎ Write

ᓂ Look at the pictures.

🕷 Say the words.

What is the beginning sound?

✎ Write the letter at the beginning of each word.

1. ___ ouse

2. ___ ircle

3. ___ indow

4. ___ ing

5. ___ ard

6. ___ itamin

7. ___ alendar

8. ___ andwich

ESL Phonics for All Ages   Book 1   © Elizabeth Claire 2007   **Test**

👓 Look and ✏ Write

👓 Look at the pictures.

🗣 Say the words.

What is the beginning sound?

✏ Write two letters at the beginning of each word.

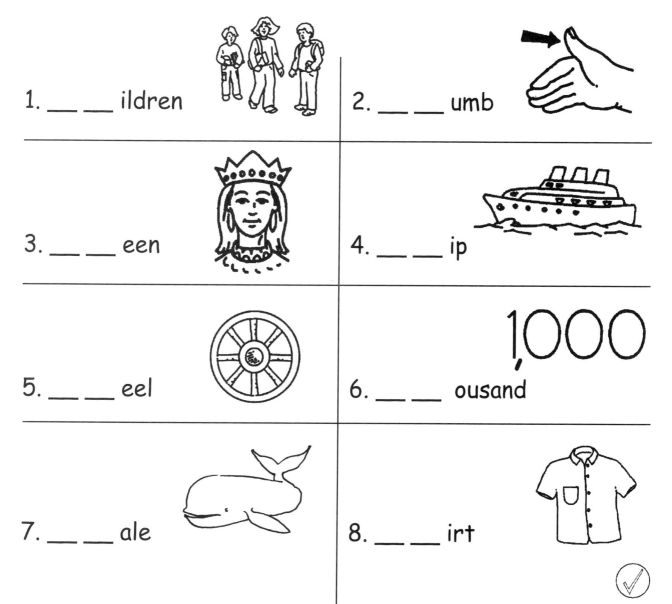

1. __ __ ildren

2. __ __ umb

3. __ __ een

4. __ __ ip

5. __ __ eel

6. __ __ ousand

7. __ __ ale

8. __ __ irt

Word List

a
all
and
are
around
at

baby
bag
ball
balloon
bananas
begin
beginning
bells
bicycle
big
bingo
bird
birthday
blue
boat
book
boots
box
boy
bus
but

calendar
can
cane
car
carrot
cat
ceiling
cent
center
chair
chalk
chant
check
cheek
cheese
cherries
chicken

children
cigar
circle
city
coat
cold
cookie
corn
cow
cup

dancer
days
deer
desk
dime
dish
do
dog
doll
dollar
door
down
draw
drawing
dream
duck

each
eating

face
family
farmer
father
fifty
find
fine
finger
fish
five
flag
foot
four
fun

game
garage
garbage
gas
general
genie
gently
giant
gift
gingerbread man
giraffe
girl
goat
good bye
gum
gym

hair
hamburger
hand
happy
has
hat
have
he
heart
hill
horse
hot
hot dog
house
how

I
I'm
is
it
it's

jack-in-the-box
jack-o'lantern
jacket
jail
jam
jar
jeans

jet
jingle
judge
jug
juice

kangaroo
kettle
key
king
kiss
kite
kitten

lamp
leaf
leg
lemon
letter
letters
life
like
likes
lion
lips
listen
lock
look
looking
lunch

mailbox
makes
man
map
mask
may
merrily
milk
mitten
mom
money
monkey
moon
mouth
my

name
neck
nest
newspaper
nickel
night
nine
nineteen
nobody
nose
notebook
number
numbers
nurse

of
oh
old
one-horse
open
or

page
pants
paper
pear
pencil
piano
picture
pie
pig
pin
playing
please
pot
puzzle

quart
quarter
queen
question mark
quilt
quiz

rabbit
radio
rain
rake
rat
read
rice
ride
road
rock
roof
row
roses
rug
ruler

salad
salt
same
sandwich
say
see
sentence
seven
shadow
shark
she
sheep
shell
ship
shirt
shoe
shovel
sing
sink
six
sleigh
so
so long
soap
sock
sofa
some
sound
soup
stream

sugar
sun
sweet

table
tea
teacher
teeth
telephone
ten
test
thank you
the
there
thermometer
these
they
thief
thirteen
thirty
this
thousand
thumb
Thursday
to
toes
tooth
toys
tuna
turtle
twenty
two

vacuum cleaner
valley
van
vase
vegetables
vest
violets
violin
visitor
vitamin
volcano
volleyball

wallet
was
washing machine
wastebasket
watch
water
way
we
welcome
whale
what
wheel
wheelbarrow
when
where
where's
whip
whisket
whistle
window
with
woman
words
write

yacht
yak
yam
yard
yarn
yawn
yellow
yo-yo
yolk
you
your

zebra
zero
zip code
zipper
zoo

My Work: (corrected)

Check your work.
Write the number that you have correct for each page.

Page	Correct / Total
4	_____ / 8
5	_____ / 6
8	_____ / 6
9	_____ / 6
12	_____ / 8
13	_____ / 6
16	_____ / 6
17	_____ / 8
20	_____ / 8
21	_____ / 6
24	_____ / 6
25	_____ / 8
26	_____ / 21
27	_____ / 8
30	_____ / 8

Page	Correct / Total
32	_____ / 6
33	_____ / 6
36	_____ / 8
38	_____ / 5
42	_____ / 8
44	_____ / 4
45	_____ / 6
48	_____ / 8
51	_____ / 6
53	_____ / 6
54	_____ / 21
59	_____ / 8
61	_____ / 6
64	_____ / 8
65	_____ / 6

Page	Correct / Total
66	_____ / 21
67	_____ / 5
70	_____ / 7
74	_____ / 7
78	_____ / 8
79	_____ / 18
82	_____ / 8
84	_____ / 6
86	_____ / 8
87	_____ / 8
88	_____ / 8
89	_____ / 8

ESL Phonics for All Ages   Book 1   © Elizabeth Claire 2007   Unit